STUDY GUIDE

RICK WARREN

40 DAYS OF COMMUNITY

WHAT ON EARTH ARE WE HERE FOR?

ZONDERVAN®
.com

ZONDERVAN.com/
AUTHORTRACKER
follow your favorite authors

ZONDERVAN

40 Days of Community Study Guide
Copyright © 2012 by Rick Warren

This title is also available as a Zondervan ebook. Visit www.zondervan.com/ebooks.

Requests for information should be addressed to:
Zondervan, *Grand Rapids, Michigan* 49530

ISBN 978-0-310-68911-9

Scripture quotations marked CEV are taken from the *Contemporary English Version*. Copyright © 1995 by American Bible Society. Used by permission.

Scripture quotations marked ESV are taken from *The Holy Bible, English Standard Version*, copyright © 2001 by Crossway Bible, a division of Good News Publishers. Used by permission. All rights reserved.

Scripture quotations marked GNB are taken from the *Good News Bible*, Second Edition. Copyright © 1992 by American Bible Society. All rights reserved.

Scripture quotations marked GW are taken from the *God's Word®️ Translation*. Copyright © 1995 by God's Word to the Nations. Published by Green Key Books. Used by permission.

Scripture quotations marked LB are taken from *The Living Bible*. Copyright © 1971 by Tyndale House Publishers, Inc., Wheaton, Illinois. All rights reserved.

Scripture quotations marked MSG are taken from *The Message*. Copyright © 1993, 1994, 1995, 1996, 2000, 2001, 2002. Used by permission of NavPress Publishing Group.

Scripture quotations marked NASB are taken from the *New American Standard Bible*. Copyright © 1960, 1962, 1963, 1968, 1971, 1972, 1973, 1975, 1977, 1995 by The Lockman Foundation. Used by permission.

Scripture quotations marked NCV are taken from the *Holy Bible, New Century Version*. Copyright © 1987, 1988, 1991 by Word Publishing, a division of Thomas Nelson, Inc. Used by permission.

Scripture quotations marked NIV are taken from the Holy Bible, *New International Version®️, NIV®️*. Copyright © 1973, 1978, 1984 by Biblica, Inc.™️ Used by permission of Zondervan. All rights reserved worldwide.

Scripture quotations marked NJB are taken from *The New Jerusalem Bible*, copyright © 1985 Darton, Longman & Todd, Ltd. and Doubleday, a division of Bantam Doubleday Dell Publishing Group, Inc., Garden City, N.Y.

Scripture quotations marked NKJV are taken from the New King James Version. Copyright © 1982, by Thomas Nelson, Inc. Used by permission. All rights reserved.

Scripture quotations marked NLT are taken from the *Holy Bible, New Living Translation*, copyright © 1996, 2004. Used by permission of Tyndale House Publishers, Inc., Wheaton, Illinois. All rights reserved.

Scripture quotations marked TEV are taken from *Today's English Version*. Copyright © American Bible Society 1966, 1971, 1976, 1992.

Any Internet addresses (websites, blogs, etc.) and telephone numbers in this book are offered as a resource. They are not intended in any way to be or imply an endorsement by Zondervan, nor does Zondervan vouch for the content of these sites and numbers for the life of this book.

Cover design: Ron Huizinga
Interior design: Matthew Van Zomeren and Ben Fetterley

Printed in the United States of America

12 13 14 15 16 17 /DCI/ 25 24 23 22 21 20 19 18 17 16 15 14 13 12 11 10 9 8 7 6 5 4 3 2 1

CONTENTS

INTRODUCTION

Dear Friends,

If you have read *The Purpose Driven® Life*, you have discovered that God placed each of us on earth for five purposes: to get to know and love him (worship), to learn to love each other (fellowship), to grow in becoming like Jesus (discipleship), to practice using our talents in serving God (ministry), and to share the good news with others (evangelism). Today, millions of people around the world have begun to enjoy living a purpose driven life.

But this life of purpose that God intends for you is not meant to be lived alone. In fact, it is impossible to fulfill God's five purposes for your life by yourself. We need each other! From the beginning, God's plan has been that you will fulfill his purposes in community with other people—people in your church family, in your small group, and in the world around you. Why did God plan it this way? Because we're better together!

The goal of *40 Days of Community* is to water the seeds of purpose that may have been planted in your life through reading *The Purpose Driven Life*, and help you take the next step to spiritual maturity and a meaningful life on earth. *40 Days of Community* will deepen your understanding of how God uses other people—specifically others in your church family—for your good and your growth. It will also show you how God can use you to bless others.

Our focus for the next forty days will be on fulfilling God's five purposes together. We'll do this in two ways: first, by deepening the community of love within our church family, and second, by reaching out in love to the community around our church family. Both are essential for a healthy, balanced, purpose driven life.

Your participation in this small group will be the most essential part of *40 Days of Community*. Real community is caught, not taught. In your group, you'll not just learn how to build community—hopefully, you'll experience it.

The Purpose Driven Life focused on the question: "What on earth am I here for?" In *40 Days of Community*, we're looking at a different question: "What on earth are *we* here for?" During the next six weeks, we'll examine the five reasons we need each other to fulfill God's purposes for our lives. Here's an overview of the reasons:

We fellowship better together! The Bible says you were formed for fellowship, and obviously you can't fellowship by yourself! It takes at least two people. At the same time, you can't fellowship with a crowd either. True fellowship happens in a small group of people. That's why Jesus had a small group of twelve disciples! He modeled fellowship.

Community doesn't happen automatically. And joining a church doesn't guarantee fellowship! You can attend church services your entire life and still feel lonely and disconnected. The Bible says, *"You must learn to be considerate of one another, cultivating a life in common"* (1 Corinthians 1:10 MSG). Notice that fellowship is something we must learn how to do. It must be intentionally cultivated.

What does it mean to cultivate a life in common? In the Bible, the Greek word for fellowship is *koinonia*. It means to be as committed to each other as we are to Jesus Christ. Real fellowship takes us beyond simply socializing or studying together and into deeper levels of serving together and, at times, even suffering together. That kind of fellowship is the antidote to the pervasive loneliness that haunts so many people.

We grow better together! Just as your hand can't grow if it gets severed from your body, you cannot grow spiritually if you are detached from fellowship with a local body of believers. The Bible says that together we are the body of Christ. And as such, every member of the body is important and necessary for the body to function as it was designed to do.

During *40 Days of Community* we'll practice some of the best ways to help each other grow spiritually, such as accepting each other (Romans 15:7), affirming each other (1 Thessalonians 5:11), and advising each other (Colossians 3:16). Just as a baby needs a family in order to grow, you need a spiritual family in order to become all God intends for you to become.

Some people think that the only way to be holy or righteous is to live in isolation—become a hermit in a cave so you won't be stained by humanity. But Jesus, the most holy person who ever lived, lived among us—in the middle of all our problems. He comforted the poor, hung out with outcasts, touched lepers, and associated with people with all kinds of hang-ups and bad habits. Religious leaders called him "the friend of sinners," a derogatory term, but Jesus considered it evidence of his love.

It's only in community that we learn life's most important lesson—learning how to love. Without relationships, we'll never be able to develop patience, kindness, unselfishness, forgiveness, and all the other Christlike qualities that God wants us to possess.

We serve better together! Paul urged the believers in the church at Philippi, *"Then make me truly happy by agreeing wholeheartedly with each other, loving one another, and working together with one heart and purpose"* (Philippians 2:2 NLT). There are many benefits to serving God together instead of by yourself: we compensate for each other's weaknesses, we're more efficient, we multiply our effectiveness, we can defeat bigger problems, and we can support each other when we're tired or discouraged.

Did you know that your talents are not for your benefit? God gave them to you for the benefit of others. And he gave others talents for your benefit. That way, none of us can arrogantly claim that we are completely self-sufficient. God wants us to depend on each other to accomplish his purposes.

In fact, our talents are best used when we combine them with the talents of others. As the Bible says, *"Two people can accomplish more than twice as much as one; they get a better return for their labor"* (Ecclesiastes 4:9 NLT). Serving God together is the way he intended, and during *40 Days of Community*, many of us will experience the joy of serving together for the very first time.

We worship better together! Worshiping together increases our joy, enlarges our perspective, helps others to believe, and guarantees God's presence in our midst. Jesus said, *"Whenever two or three of you come together in my name, I am there with you"* (Matthew 18:20 CEV). While it is true that God is always with us, there is a unique and powerful sense of his presence that can only be enjoyed and experienced in community with other believers.

When we worship with other believers it helps us see beyond ourselves and our own problems. C. S. Lewis, the brilliant Oxford author, was asked about the importance of worshiping together. He told about his first experience in attending worship services: "I very much disliked their hymns, which I considered to be fifth-rate poems set to sixth-rate music. But as I went on, I saw the great merit of it all ... and gradually my conceit began peeling off. I realized that the sixth-rate hymns were, nevertheless, being sung with devotion and benefit by an old saint in elastic-side boots in the opposite pew, and I realized that I wasn't fit to clean those boots. Worshiping together gets us out of our solitary conceit."

We reach out better together! The Bible says, *"Above all else, live in a way that brings honor to the good news about Christ.... Then I will know that you are working together and struggling side by side to get others to believe the good news"* (Philippians 1:27 CEV). God expects us to partner in sharing the good news with others.

One practical way you can do this is by inviting people from your community to be a part of this small group study with you! Many people who might be reluctant or hesitant to visit a church service would gladly accept an invitation to an informal group study in a home or office. Don't miss this perfect opportunity to reach out to neighbors, friends, and coworkers.

Another way your small group can reach out together is through a group outreach project. There are plenty of opportunities right in your own community: the poor who need to be fed, shut-ins who need a visit, the elderly who could use some help around the house with repairs or yard work, kids with a single parent who need mentors, and people all around you who need to know that God loves them and has a purpose for their lives. That's why he sent Jesus to die for them.

Jesus tells us in Matthew 25:35–40 (NIV) that one day we'll each stand before God and one of the things we'll be evaluated on is how we treated other people: *"I was hungry and you gave me something to eat, I was thirsty and you gave me something to drink, I was a stranger and you invited me in, I needed clothes and you clothed me, I was sick and you looked after me, I was in prison and you came to visit me."* We'll say, "When did we do that to you, Lord?" And God will reply, *"Whatever you did for one of the least of these . . . you did for me."*

It's time for us to put our love into action. Imagine what could happen if every small group in your church reached out together, showing love in practical ways to those in your community. Don't you think that would make a difference in your area?

Now imagine what could happen if every small group in all the purpose driven churches across the country did it with you! Millions of lives would be touched, millions of people would begin a relationship with Christ, millions of practical needs would be met, and the church would become known more for the love it shows than for what it is against. God would be pleased, and we could see a spiritual awakening that is desperately needed in our culture.

God is moving in amazing ways in thousands of churches these days. I invite you to be a part of making history! It is an invitation to become a part of a great movement of purpose driven people and churches who are living for the global glory of God. Someone once pointed out that snowflakes are frail, but when enough of them stick together they can stop traffic. In the same way, you and I may feel like we can't make much of a difference as individuals. But together—with others in your small group, and with your church family, and with other congregations that are also committed to God's purposes—we can make a difference in our culture and our world. That is the awesome power of community!

It is no accident that you are a part of *40 Days of Community*. Before you were born, God chose you to be a difference-maker and to make an impact for good with your life. Are you willing to take the next step in growing a life of purpose and meaning? Then let's join together for this forty-day spiritual journey—deepening the community of love within your church and reaching out in love to the community around your church.

We are better together!

With love and admiration for you,

[signature: Rick Warren]

This *40 Days of Community* study guide contains:

- Six weekly sessions based on my teaching in the *40 Days of Community* video

- Memory verses and discussion questions

- Weekly group activities oriented around God's five purposes

- Group development resources to equip the group host and members to experience a successful small group study

Be sure to bring this study guide with you for each small group meeting. During these next forty days, I urge you to cut back on television intake and any other activities that could distract you from getting the most out of this journey together.

UNDERSTANDING YOUR STUDY GUIDE

You are about to embark on a life-changing experience in your small group. Studying God's Word together always impacts our lives in powerful ways. One of the unique features of this curriculum is that it uses God's five purposes for your life as the format for each session. These purposes, as found in *The Purpose Driven Life*, are Fellowship, Discipleship, Ministry, Mission, and Worship. When you see the following symbols and elements in the study guide, you will know the particular purpose that section promotes. The format of each session is as follows:

Connect Together: Intimate connection with God and his family is the foundation for spiritual growth. This section will help you get to know the members of your group. It will also give you the opportunity to check your progress from week to week.

Grow Together: This section is made up of three components:

- A weekly Bible memory verse that fits the theme of the session.

- A weekly video teaching session by Pastor Rick Warren. Follow along using the outline in this study guide.

- Discussion questions designed to facilitate a deeper understanding of the Bible and to help you consider how the truths of Scripture can impact your life.

Serve Together: Nothing is more fulfilling than using your God-given gifts to serve the needs of others in God's family. This section will help your group discover how you can serve each other and your church together.

Share Together: God wants to use your small group to reach your community for Christ. The Share Together section is designed to give you and your group practical suggestions and exercises for sharing the love of Christ with others.

Worship Together: In each small group session you will have the opportunity to surrender your hearts to God and express your worship to him. In this section you will be led in various forms of small group worship including prayer, Scripture reading, singing together, and sharing what God is doing in your lives. This portion of your session can be very meaningful for your group.

Host Tips: These brief instructions in gray boxes are helpful coaching hints for your group host. Here's your first ...

> **Host Tip:** The study guide material is meant to be your servant, not your master. So please don't feel you have to answer every question in every section. The point is not to race through the session; the point is to take time to let God work in your lives. Nor is it necessary to "go around the circle" before you move on to the next question. Give people the freedom to speak, but don't insist that they do. Your group will enjoy deeper, more open sharing and discussion if people don't feel pressured to speak up. If your group is unable to work through all the material in a session, we have recommended one question or activity with an asterisk (*) in each section of the study.

How to Use This Video Curriculum

Here is a brief explanation of the features on your small group DVD. These features include six Helps for Hosts, one Group Lifter, and six Video Teaching Sessions. Here's how they work:

Helps for Hosts are special video messages just for group hosts. They provide brief video instruction from Pastor Rick Warren that will help you, the host, prepare for each week's small group session. The group host should watch these features before the group arrives for each study.

The **Group Lifter** is an introductory message to your whole group from Pastor Rick Warren. Be sure to show this Group Lifter to your group before you watch the video teaching for session one.

The **Video Teaching Sessions** provide your group with the teaching for each week of the study. Watch these features with your group. After watching the video teaching, continue in your study by working through the discussion questions and activities in the study guide.

Follow these simple steps for a successful small group session:

1. *Hosts:* Before your group arrives, watch the Helps for Hosts feature by Pastor Rick Warren. This brief video message will help you prepare for your small group session.
2. *Group:* Open your group meeting by using the Connect Together section in your study guide.
3. *Group:* Watch Pastor Rick's video teaching and follow along in the outlines in the study guide.
4. *Group:* Complete the rest of the discussion materials for each session in the study guide.

It's just that simple. Have a great study together!

WHAT MATTERS MOST

Connect Together
10 minutes

> **Host Tip:** If your group is unable to work through the entire session, we have recommended one question or activity with an asterisk (*) in each section of the study.

*1. Give everyone a chance to introduce themselves and share how they came to be a part of this group.

2. Open to the Purpose Driven Group Guidelines in the Small Group Resources section of your study guide, page 79. Take a few minutes to review these group guidelines before you begin this *40 Days of Community* study. These guidelines will help everyone know what to expect from the group and how to contribute to a meaningful small group experience.

3. Love is defined in many ways by our culture. How would you define love?

Grow Together
55 minutes

Memory Verse

"Your love for one another will prove to the world that you are my disciples."

John 13:35 NLT

Watch the session one video now and fill in the blanks in the outline on pages 19–21. Refer back to the outline during your discussion time.

WHAT MATTERS MOST

If you are a follower of Christ Jesus ... all that matters is your faith that makes you love others.

Galatians 5:6 CEV

If I speak in the tongues of men and of angels, but have not love, I am only a resounding gong or a clanging cymbal. ²If I have the gift of prophecy and can fathom all mysteries and all knowledge, and if I have a faith that can move mountains, but have not love, I am nothing. ³If I give all I possess to the poor and surrender my body to the flames, but have not love, I gain nothing.

⁴Love is patient, love is kind. It does not envy, it does not boast, it is not proud. ⁵It is not rude, it is not self-seeking, it is not easily angered, it keeps no record of wrongs. ⁶Love does not delight in evil but rejoices with the truth. ⁷It always protects, always trusts, always hopes, always perseveres.

⁸Love never fails. But where there are prophecies, they will cease; where there are tongues, they will be stilled; where there is knowledge, it will pass away. ⁹For we know in part and we prophesy in part, ¹⁰but when perfection comes, the imperfect disappears. ¹¹When I was a child, I talked like a child, I thought like a child, I reasoned like a child. When I became a man, I put childish ways behind me. ¹²Now we see but a poor reflection as in a mirror; then we shall see face to face. Now I know in part; then I shall know fully, even as I am fully known.

¹³And now these three remain: faith, hope and love. But the greatest of these is love.

1 Corinthians 13:1 – 13 NIV

FIVE RADICAL STATEMENTS ABOUT LOVE

If I don't live a life of love:

1. Nothing I ____*say*____ will matter.

If I could speak in any language in heaven or on earth, but didn't love others, I would only be making meaningless noise like a loud gong or a clanging cymbal.

1 Corinthians 13:1 NLT

2. Nothing I ___*know*___ will matter.

I may have the gift of prophecy. I may understand all the secret things of God and have all knowledge.... But if I do not have love, then I am nothing.

1 Corinthians 13:2 NCV

3. Nothing I ___*believe*___ will matter.

Even if I had the gift of faith so that I could speak to a mountain and make it move, I would still be worth nothing at all without love.

1 Corinthians 13:2b LB

4. Nothing I ___*give*___ will matter.

If I gave everything I have to the poor and even sacrificed my body ... but if I didn't love others, I would be of no value whatsoever.

1 Corinthians 13:3 NLT

5. Nothing I ___*accomplish*___ will matter.

No matter what I say, what I believe, or what I do, I'm bankrupt without love.

1 Corinthians 13:3b MSG

What Is Love?

- Love is a ___*command*___.

"A new command I give you: Love one another. As I have loved you, so you must love one another."

John 13:34 NIV

• Love is a ___choice___.

Go after a life of love as if your life depended on it—because it does.
1 Corinthians 14:1 MSG

• Love is a ___conduct___.

Let us stop just saying we love people; let us really love them and show it by our actions.
1 John 3:18 LB

• Love is a ___commitment___.

God is love. If we keep on loving others, we will stay one in our hearts with God and he will stay one with us.
1 John 4:16b CEV

Discussion Questions

*1. First Corinthians 13:1–3 makes five radical statements about love. They are the first five fill-ins of your outline. Which statement strikes you the most? Why?

2. First Corinthians 14:1 (MSG) says, *"Go after a life of love as if your life depended on it—because it does."* On a practical, day-to-day level, what does it mean to "go after a life of love"? What are some steps you can take to live this way?

SERVE TOGETHER
10 minutes

*1. One way to "go after" a life of love is to show appreciation to others. Is there a worker in your church who needs to be shown appreciation? As a group, choose either a church staff member or volunteer whom you could affirm this week. You might select an usher, a janitor, a teacher, a secretary, or a youth worker—someone who is involved in serving your congregation. Discuss ways your group can show love and appreciation to that person this week, such as a gift certificate to their favorite store or restaurant, a thank-you card signed by all the members of your group, tickets to a ball game, etc. Recruit one or two volunteers from your group to handle the details. Then, as a group, make plans to present your appreciation gift to the person you chose.

SHARE TOGETHER
15 minutes

*1a. Use the Circles of Life diagram on page 81 to help you think of a neighbor, family member, friend, or coworker who would benefit from joining your small group.

1b. Choose a person on your Circles of Life diagram to whom you can show the love of Christ this week—someone you have been meaning to call or visit, or someone you need to invite to church. Commit to doing something for that person this week. Tell your small group who the person is and what you will do: send an email, make a call, write a letter, buy a little gift, take him out for coffee, or invite her to join your small group next week.

2. At the end of his message, Pastor Rick asked you to begin discussing a project your whole group can do together to reach out to your community with the love of Christ, particularly in the areas of assisting the poor, caring for the sick, and reaching the lost. This project will become a major focus for your group over the next forty days. Your church may choose to focus on one big project together, or you may decide to do this on a group-by-group basis. Our hope is that by the end of this *40 Days of Community* study, every small group in your church will have begun an outreach project in your town. We'll talk about this in greater detail next week, but we just want to get it on your radar screen in this session. Start discussing the idea right now. Why is it important for you as a group to reach out to your community?

WORSHIP TOGETHER

10 minutes

> **Host Tip:** To maximize prayer time and allow greater opportunity for personal sharing, break into subgroups of three or four people. This is especially important if your small group has more than eight members.

1. In simple, one-sentence prayers take a few moments to thank God for his love. If praying aloud with people is new or awkward for you, feel free to pray silently.

*2. One of the best ways to show each other love is to pray for each other. Share your prayer requests with your small group and then take time to pray together. Be sure to pray for friends and loved ones who do not have a personal relationship with God through Jesus Christ. Record your prayer requests on the Small Group Prayer and Praise Report beginning on page 82 of this study guide. Keeping track of group prayer requests and answers to prayer would be a great job for someone in your group. Any volunteers?

BEFORE YOU LEAVE

1. Take a few minutes to look at the Small Group Calendar in the Small Group Resources section, page 87 of this study guide. Healthy groups share responsibilities and group ownership. Fill out the calendar together, noting where you will meet each week, who will facilitate your discussion time, and who will provide a meal or snack. Note special events, such as birthdays, anniversaries, socials, etc. Coordinating these details would be another great job for someone in the group.

2. Collect phone numbers and email addresses from your small group members. The group roster (called My Small Group) on page 90 of your study guide is a good place to keep this information. Pass your study guides around the circle and have your group members fill in their contact information.

3. Here is a ministry someone in your small group can take responsibility for: organize an email prayer hotline. This is a great way for your group members to share prayer requests and answers to prayer between your small group gatherings. When a need for prayer arises, just call or email your email prayer hotline coordinator. The coordinator will then email the entire small group with either a prayer alert of your request or with a praise report of God's answer to your prayers.

REACHING OUT TOGETHER

Connect Together
10 minutes

Host Tip: If your group is unable to work through the entire session, we have recommended one question or activity with an asterisk (*) in each section of the study.

1. Welcome any people who are new to your group this week.

*2. Check your progress on last week's group assignment to show love and appreciation to a church staff member or volunteer.

3. How are you progressing with your personal commitment from last week to reach out to someone with the love of Jesus Christ? Did you get started? If so, how did it go?

4. Would anyone like to tell the group about an answer to prayer or something they are learning from their *40 Days of Community Devotional* readings? Be sure to record answers to prayer in the Small Group Prayer and Praise Report beginning on page 82 of this study guide.

Grow Together
55 minutes

Memory Verse

Be wise in the way you act with people who are not believers, making the most of every opportunity.

Colossians 4:5 NCV

Watch the session two video now and fill in the blanks in the outline on pages 29–30. Refer back to the outline during your discussion time.

REACHING OUT TOGETHER

Love is kind.

1 Corinthians 13:4 NIV

[The disciples said to Jesus,] "Send the people away so they can go to the surrounding countryside and villages and buy themselves something to eat." ³⁷But Jesus answered, "You give them something to eat." They said to him, "That would take eight months of a man's wages! Are we to go and spend that much on bread and give it to them to eat?" ³⁸"How many loaves do you have?" he asked. "Go and see." When they found out, they said, "Five—and two fish." ³⁹Then Jesus directed them to have all the people sit down in groups ... of hundreds and fifties. ⁴¹Taking the five loaves and the two fish and looking up to heaven, he gave thanks and broke the loaves. Then he gave them to his disciples to set before the people. He also divided the two fish among them all. ⁴²They all ate and were satisfied, ⁴³and the disciples picked up twelve basketfuls of broken pieces of bread and fish. ⁴⁴The number of the men who had eaten was five thousand.

Mark 6:36–44 NIV

MEETING THE NEEDS OF OTHERS

- Recognize the ___*need*___.

- Take ___*inventory*___.

My grace is sufficient for you, for my power is made perfect in weakness.

2 Corinthians 12:9 NIV

- Get _____*organized*_____.

- Measure the _____*need*_____.

- Prepare your _____*heart*_____.

God will give you much, so that you can give away much, and when we take your gifts to those who need them they will break out into thanksgiving and praise to God for your help.

2 Corinthians 9:11 LB

- Be _____*available*_____.

Do not merely listen to the word, and so deceive yourselves. Do what it says.

James 1:22 NIV

Those you help will be glad not only because of your generous gifts to themselves and to others, but they will praise God for this proof that your deeds are as good as your doctrine.

2 Corinthians 9:13 LB

DISCUSSION QUESTIONS

Host Tip: If your group has eight or more members, we suggest you break into subgroups of three or four people for greater participation and deeper discussion. At the end of the discussion time, come back together and have someone from each group report on the highlights of their discussions.

Host Tip: This week there are just two questions in this section because we want you to spend most of your discussion time working on the Share Together section of the study.

1. James 1:22 tells us it's not enough just to know truth. We have to put it into practice. And 2 Corinthians 9:13 (LB) says our deeds should be *"as good as [our] doctrine."* What does this mean on a practical level? How do these truths relate to sharing your faith?

*2. Pastor Rick said, "God wants to use your small group to reach the world for Jesus Christ. If you want to know God's plan for solving the world's problems look around the room. You're it. You are God's plan.... God works through his people—through physical, tangible demonstrations of compassion, mercy, and care." What do you think about that statement? Does it excite you, scare you, or overwhelm you? Why?

Host Tip: There will be no Serve Together questions this week. We want you to focus the rest of your time on the Share Together section of your study.

Share Together
25 minutes

God wants to use your small group to reach out to the world for Jesus Christ. To discover how, follow the six steps from Pastor Rick's message this week:

*1. **Recognize the need.** What physical and spiritual needs do people have in your community? Your church may have established a *Better Together* missions project team to explore church-wide outreach opportunities in your community. If your church has such a team, look over their local missions opportunity report. If your church is planning one big, church-wide project, talk about the role your group will play in that project. Otherwise, use the list below to help spur creative thinking in your group for a local outreach idea. As a group, decide what your project will be.

Small Group Outreach Ideas:
- Volunteer at a local food bank once a month.
- Divide into teams and rotate weekly visits to a shut-in or nursing home.
- Start a weekly sports program for the kids who live near your church.
- Divide into teams and rotate weekly volunteer service at a homeless shelter.
- Partner with a prison or jail ministry to start a small group using the book *The Purpose Driven Life*.
- Assist in a local HIV/AIDS ministry outreach.
- Volunteer in an after-school tutoring program for kids who are at risk of dropping out of school.

2. **Take inventory.** What talents, abilities, experiences, and resources are available in your group to help meet the need you have selected?

3. **Get organized.** Determine how much time your project will take and what kind of resources will be required. Make a plan. Figure out a timeline, divide up responsibilities, and assign tasks.

4. **Measure the need.** Pastor Rick said, "You'll never know what God can do through you until you come to the end of yourself—until you face a hungry crowd with only a sack lunch." Is your project a big enough challenge to your faith? If not, why not?

5 & 6. **Prepare your heart** and **Be available.** We will talk about these last two points in the Worship Together section.

 WORSHIP TOGETHER
10 minutes

1. **Prepare your heart.** The Bible says in 1 Chronicles 29:14 that everything we have was given to us by God. In silent or spoken prayer, thank God for what he has given you and then offer it back to him to do with as he will.

*2. **Be available.** Romans 12:1 tells us to worship God by offering our bodies to him as living sacrifices. In prayer, offer yourselves to God. Ask him to give you strength and courage to step out in faith as you join together in your community outreach project.

3. **Pray for each other's prayer requests.** Pray especially for the people you are inviting to come to your small group or church with you. Be sure your prayer coordinator records the group's prayer requests on the Small Group Prayer and Praise Report beginning on page 82 of this study guide.

BEFORE YOU LEAVE

Was anyone missing from your group this week? If someone was absent, ask for a volunteer from the group to call or email that person and let them know they were missed. It's very important for people to know they are cared about.

BELONGING TOGETHER

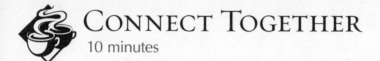

Connect Together
10 minutes

> **Host Tip:** If your group is unable to work through the entire session, we have recommended one question or activity with an asterisk (*) in each section of the study.

*1. Check your progress on your small group outreach project. Are your plans coming together? Are there any loose ends that need to be tied down?

2. Who has blessed you by meeting a practical need in your life? How did their kindness make you feel?

Grow Together
45 minutes

Memory Verse

Since we are all one body in Christ, we belong to each other, and each of us needs all the others.

Romans 12:5b NLT

Watch the session three video now and fill in the blanks in the outline on pages 37. Refer back to the outline during your discussion time.

Belonging Together

Two are better than one, because they have a good return for their work: ¹⁰If one falls down, his friend can help him up. But pity the man who falls and has no one to help him up!... ¹²Though one may be overpowered, two can defend themselves. A cord of three strands is not quickly broken.

Ecclesiastes 4:9–12 NIV

Lessons on Love from 1 Corinthians 13:7

• Love always _protects_.

A gossip betrays a confidence but a trustworthy man keeps a secret.

Proverbs 11:13 NIV

Protects = _cover over with silence_

• Love always _trusts_.

We believe _in_ each other ... we believe _for_ each other.

• Love always _hopes_.

Be _enthusiastic_ about other people's accomplishments.

• Love always _perseveres_.

Some friendships do not last, but some friends are more loyal than brothers.

Proverbs 18:24 GNB

In Christ, we who are many form one body, and each member belongs to all the others.

Romans 12:5 NIV

DISCUSSION QUESTIONS

Host Tip: If your group has eight or more members, we suggest you break into subgroups of three or four people for greater participation and deeper discussion.

For this week's study, please break into separate groups for men and women.

*1. Which of the four statements about love from 1 Corinthians 13:7 spoke to you most powerfully? Why? How can you apply these truths to your personal life this week?

2. What can we do to apply these truths to our group life? What does it mean to really trust each other and to persevere in our relationships together? What can we do to build trust and foster hope within our group?

3. Talk about a time when you needed the faith of your friends to lift you in prayer, or a time when God answered your prayers for someone else.

4. Have one or two group members share their story of how they came to Christ and the role friendship played in their decision.

 # SERVE TOGETHER
10 minutes

*1. A recent survey revealed that the number one characteristic of a growing church is the atmosphere of love among the membership. How would you describe the atmosphere of love in your church (welcoming, warm, safe, impersonal, cliquey, etc.)? What can your small group do to help build a more loving community in your church?

2. Have you made a membership commitment to your church? If not, what is holding you back?

 Share Together
45 minutes

1. Your group outreach project can be a great conversation starter for inviting seekers as well as Christ-following friends to join your small group. When people express interest or curiosity about your project, invite them to join you at your next group meeting to find out more about it. Who can you tell about your group outreach project this week?

*2. Think of a friend who is not currently connected to a church. Why not invite that person to come to church with you this weekend? What is the worst thing that could happen if you invite them? What is the best thing that could happen if you invite them? Is the potential benefit worth the risk? Remember, over 90 percent of Christians first went to church because a friend or family member invited them. Tell your group the name of at least one person who you will invite to church or to your next small group meeting.

Name _____

Name _____

WORSHIP TOGETHER
10 minutes

1. Would anyone like to share an answer to a prayer from last week? Be sure to record answers to prayer in the Small Group Prayer and Praise Report beginning on page 82 of this study guide.

2. Pray for your small group outreach project.

*3. Love requires us to believe *in* each other and *for* each other. Pair up with a spiritual partner for the rest of your prayer time. A spiritual partner is someone we can talk to about our spiritual growth and "call for back-up" when we need prayer support. Take a moment to select someone in your group to be your spiritual partner for the remaining weeks of this study. (We strongly recommend that men partner with men, and women partner with women.) After you have paired up, pray for each other's requests. Plan to check in with each other by phone, email, or over coffee at least once before your next small group meeting. This could be a great time to pray for each other during the coming week, and share what you are learning from your *40 Days of Community Devotional* reading.

Growing
Together

Connect Together
10 minutes

> **Host Tip:** If your group is unable to work through the entire session, we have recommended one question or activity with an asterisk (*) in each section of the study.

1. Have you had a chance to invite a friend to church or to your small group yet? How did they respond?

*2. Check the progress of your group outreach project.

3. Who have been some of the greatest examples of Christian love for you?

Grow Together
50 minutes

Memory Verse

Encourage one another and build each other up.

　　　　　　　　　　　　　　　　1 Thessalonians 5:11 NIV

Watch the session four video now and fill in the blanks in the outline on pages 45–47. Refer back to the outline during your discussion time.

GROWING TOGETHER

1. Growing together requires __patience__.

Love is patient.... ⁵It is not rude ... it is not easily angered.
> 1 Corinthians 13:4–5 NIV

Be humble and gentle in every way. Be patient with each other and lovingly accept each other.
> Ephesians 4:2 GW

2. Growing together requires __truthfulness__.

Love rejoices in the truth.
> 1 Corinthians 13:6a CEV

Speak the truth in a spirit of love.
> Ephesians 4:15 TEV

SPEAKING THE TRUTH IN LOVE

- Check your __motives__.

"Why worry about a speck in your friend's eye when you have a log in your own?... ⁵First get rid of the log in your own eye; then perhaps you will see well enough to deal with the speck in your friend's eye."
> Matthew 7:3–5 NLT

- Plan your __presentation__.

  Plan __what__ you'll say it.

The right word at the right time is like precious gold set in silver.
> Proverbs 25:11 CEV

Plan _____*what*_____ you'll say.

A wise friend's kind reprimand is like a gold ring slipped on your finger.

Proverbs 25:12 MSG

Plan _____*how*_____ you'll say it.

Thoughtless words can wound as deeply as any sword, but wisely spoken words can heal.

Proverbs 12:18 TEV

• _____*Pray*_____.

• Say it _____*tactfully*_____.

A wise mature person is known for his understanding. The more pleasant his words, the more persuasive he is.

Proverbs 16:21 TEV

• Say it _____*lovingly*_____.

• Say it _____*gently*_____.

A soft answer turns away wrath.

Proverbs 15:1a NKJV

If someone is trapped in sin, you should gently lead that person back to the right path.

Galatians 6:1 CEV

An honest answer is a sign of a true friendship.

Proverbs 24:26 TEV

3. Growing together requires _____ patience _____ forgiveness
truthfulness

Love keeps no record of wrongs.

1 Corinthians 13:5b NIV

Bear with each other and forgive whatever grievances you may have against one another. Forgive as the Lord forgave you.

Colossians 3:13 NIV

"In the same way you judge others, you will be judged, and with the measure you use, it will be measured to you."

Matthew 7:2 NIV

DISCUSSION QUESTIONS

Host Tip: If your group has eight or more members, we suggest you break into subgroups of three or four people for greater participation and deeper discussion. At the end of the discussion time, come back together and have someone from each group report on the highlights of their discussions.

*1. This lesson covered three aspects of love that can sometimes be very difficult: patience, truthfulness, and forgiveness. Which part of the lesson was most meaningful to you? Why?

2. Where does impatience show up in your life?

3. What is the difference between judging people and confronting them in love?

4. How do you respond when someone hurts you? Why is it so hard to forgive people who hurt us? What are the consequences of choosing not to forgive?

SERVE TOGETHER
10 minutes

1. In what ways do patience, truthfulness, and forgiveness impact your ability to serve in ministry?

*2. Is there someone in your church or small group with whom you need to seek reconciliation? Why wait any longer? Reach out to that person this week with truthfulness and forgiveness. We will pray together about these relationships during the Worship Together section of this study.

SHARE TOGETHER
10 minutes

*1. How can unforgiveness or resentment in your relationship with someone who is not a follower of Christ affect their openness to Jesus Christ? What difference could a healed relationship make in that person's life?

2. How do unity and love in your church affect your church's testimony to your community?

 # WORSHIP TOGETHER
10 minutes

1. As Pastor Rick closed his message, he asked: "Do you need to be patient with someone? Do you need to speak the truth in love to someone? Do you need to forgive someone?" Take a moment to quietly reflect on these questions. Write down a name or a situation that comes to mind.

Name or Situation _____

*2. Break into subgroups of three or four people, or pair up with your spiritual partner. Tell each other if you have a relationship that needs healing, either through patience, truthfulness, or forgiveness. This is not a time to share details or assign blame. Simply mention the person's name or the nature of the relationship (e.g., brother, colleague, mother, neighbor, friend, etc.). Share as openly as you feel comfortable so the group can pray more specifically for you. Then, as an act of worship and because it will please the Father, pray for each other, asking God to soften your hearts and give you courage and grace to initiate the healing process. If you are not yet ready to reconcile, then pray that God will help you to become "willing to be ready."

BEFORE YOU LEAVE

Recruit a volunteer to be your group ministry project coordinator! His or her job will be to contact your church this week and ask for some practical suggestions as to how your small group can serve your church. You will need this information for next week's small group meeting.

SERVING
TOGETHER

Connect Together
10 minutes

> **Host Tip:** If your group is unable to work through the entire session, we have recommended one question or activity with an asterisk (*) in each section of the study.

*1. Check the progress of your group outreach project.

2. Last week we talked and prayed about being patient with others, speaking the truth in love, and forgiveness. How did that lesson impact your life this week? Did you see any answers to your prayer?

3. This week we are going to talk about serving the Lord by serving people in your church family. What do you think are the characteristics of a true servant?

Grow Together
45 minutes

Memory Verse

By helping each other with your troubles, you truly obey the law of Christ.

Galatians 6:2 NCV

> Watch the session five video now and fill in the blanks in the outline on pages 55. Refer back to the outline during your discussion time.

SERVING TOGETHER

FOUR KEY ASPECTS OF SERVING TOGETHER

Groups that serve together:

1. Make themselves _available_ to serve.

2. Work as a _team_.

> *From him the whole body, joined and held together by every supporting ligament, grows and builds itself up in love, as each part does its work.*
>
> Ephesians 4:16 NIV

3. Think more about _Others_ than themselves.

> *Forget yourselves long enough to lend a helping hand.*
>
> Philippians 2:4 MSG

> *Consider how we may spur one another on toward love and good deeds.*
>
> Hebrews 10:24 NIV

4. Do every task with equal _dedication_.

> *"If anyone wants to be first, he must be the very last, and the servant of all."*
>
> Mark 9:35 NIV

> *He will not forget how hard you have worked for him and how you have shown your love to him by caring for other Christians.*
>
> Hebrews 6:10 NLT

Discussion Questions

1. Are you currently serving in a ministry at your church? If you are, tell the group about it.

2. Where do you find the most joy when it comes to helping others?

3. The true test of a servant heart is in how you react when you are treated like a servant. Have you ever been treated like a servant? How did it make you feel?

*4. Consider these roadblocks to ministry: time constraints, overcommitment, lack of interest, lack of confidence, lack of information. Which of these roadblocks presents the biggest obstacle for you? What can you do to avoid or overcome these barriers to ministry?

Host Tip: There will be no Share Together questions this week. We want you to focus the rest of your time on the Serve Together section of your study.

 # Serve Together

25 minutes

What can you do together as a small group to serve your church?

*1. **Determine a need:** What will your group do? Pastor Rick said, "There is nothing too small, too mundane, or too menial for a true servant." Make a list of practical needs your group can meet in your church. Here are a few examples to get you started:

- Provide meals for a family in need.
- Pray with a church member who is in the hospital.
- Assist senior adults in your church with projects around the house.
- Offer help to military families whose moms or dads are serving overseas.
- Take on a maintenance project at church such as painting or re-carpeting an office or classroom.

- Other: _____

- Other: _____

- Other: _____

Now pray together and ask the Lord what he would have you do. After you have prayed, choose the need your group will meet.

2. **Develop a plan:** How will you meet the need? When your group has chosen your ministry project, determine your plan of action, identify the tasks, and divide up the responsibilities. If you did not choose a group ministry project coordinator last week, then select someone this week to fill this crucial role. The group ministry project coordinator will help move your plan from the talking stage to the action stage.

Task to be done	Who will do it
_____	_____
_____	_____
_____	_____
_____	_____
_____	_____
_____	_____
_____	_____
_____	_____
_____	_____
_____	_____

3. **Decide on a date:** When will you take action? Get out your calendars and choose a date when your group can serve together. Make it sooner than later.

WORSHIP TOGETHER
10 minutes

*1. Pray for your group ministry project. Commit your plans to the Lord and ask him to direct your steps. Thank God in advance for what he is going to do through you as your group blesses someone in need.

2. Pray this prayer aloud together:

> Father, we want to live our lives to please you.
> We want to walk through each day depending on your power,
> looking for your hand,
> and listening for the still, small voice of your guidance.
> Use us for your kingdom's purposes.
> Nudge us into greater acts of faith.
> Call us to a deeper level of trust.
> Soften our hearts, O Lord,
> so that we may live worthy of your calling
> and fulfill your highest purposes for our lives.
> We pray these things in the name of Jesus,
> and for the glory of your kingdom.
>
> Amen.*

* Adapted from *The NIV Worship Bible*, page 1596. © 2000
The Corinthian Group. All rights reserved. Used by permission.

3. Break into subgroups and pray for one another's prayer requests.

Host Tip: A word about singing: Some people love to sing together. Some people would rather get a root canal. In this Worship Together section, we have recommended an optional, familiar song for you to sing in your group. Please don't feel obligated to use it. It is only a suggestion for groups that are comfortable singing together. If you have a guitar or keyboard player in your small group and someone who loves to lead singing, then by all means incorporate this song or others into your worship time. If singing together is awkward for your group, simply read the lyrics out loud as a prayer.

4. *Optional:* Close your worship time by singing the song, "Take My Life and Let It Be."

Take My Life and Let It Be

Take my life, and let it be
Consecrated, Lord, to Thee.
Take my moments and my days;
Let them flow in ceaseless praise,
Let them flow in ceaseless praise.

Take my silver and my gold,
Not a mite would I withhold;
Take my intellect, and use
Ev'ry power as Thou shalt choose,
Ev'ry power as Thou shalt choose.

Take my will and make it Thine;
It shall be no longer mine.
Take my heart, it is Thine own;
It shall be Thy royal throne,
It shall be Thy royal throne.

Take my love; my Lord, I pour
At Thy feet its treasure store.
Take myself, and I will be
Ever, only, all for Thee,
Ever, only, all for Thee.

Words and music by Frances Ridley Havergal. Public domain.

Before You Leave

1. Start making plans for an evening meal or a picnic with your group
   to celebrate what God has done in your lives through this *40 Days of
   Community* study. A party is an excellent opportunity for you to invite
   people who might be interested in joining your group. Talk about your
   celebration before you leave your meeting. Where will you have your
   party? When will you have it? Will it be a potluck, will someone barbe-
   cue, or will you call out for pizza? Divide up the responsibilities and then
   get ready to enjoy a great time of fellowship together. You deserve it!

2. There is just one week left in our *40 Days of Community* study. Take a few minutes for an informal evaluation of your small group experience. What has been helpful to you? What has challenged you? What would make this a better experience? How do you feel about continuing on as a group? Talk about these issues and address any concerns that might be raised.

3. If you plan to stay together as a group, spend some time talking about what your group will study next. We invite you to visit our website at *www.SaddlebackResources.com* and check out our other video-based small group studies.

WORSHIPING TOGETHER

Connect Together
10 minutes

> **Host Tip:** If your group is unable to work through the entire session, we have recommended one question or activity with an asterisk (*) in each section of the study.

*1. Check in about the progress of your group's ministry plans that you discussed last week.

2. Would anyone like to tell about an answer to prayer or something they are learning from the *40 Days of Community Devotional* readings?

3. How would your friends rate you on the generosity meter?

Scrooge   **Mother Teresa**

Generosity Meter

Grow Together
45 minutes

Memory Verse

You have six days to do your work, but the seventh day of each week is holy because it belongs to me.

Leviticus 23:3 CEV

> Watch the session six video now and fill in the blanks in the outline on pages 65–66. Refer back to the outline during your discussion time.

Worshiping Together

Six Practical Reasons for Giving

1. Giving makes me more like ___*God*___.

   "God so loved the world that he gave ..."
   John 3:16a NIV

2. Giving draws me ___*closer*___ to God.

   "Where your treasure is, there your heart will be also."
   Matthew 6:21 NIV

3. Giving is the antidote to ___*materialism*___.

   Command those who are rich in this present world not to be arrogant nor to put their hope in wealth, which is so uncertain, but to put their hope in God, who richly provides us with everything for our enjoyment. [18]Command them ... to be generous and willing to share. [19]In this way ... they may take hold of the life that is truly life.
   1 Timothy 6:17 – 19 NIV

4. Giving strengthens my ___*faith*___.

   "Bring the whole tithe to the storehouse.... Test me in this," says the Lord Almighty, "and see if I will not throw open the floodgates of heaven and pour out so much blessing that you will not have room enough for it!"
   Malachi 3:10 NIV

5. Giving is an investment for ___*eternity*___.

   Give happily to those in need, always being ready to share ... whatever God has given you. [19]By doing this, you will be storing up real treasure for yourself in heaven — it is the only safe investment for eternity.
   1 Timothy 6:18 – 19 LB

6. Giving blesses me in _____return_____.

A generous man will prosper; he who refreshes others will himself be refreshed.

Proverbs 11:25 NIV

There is more happiness in giving than in receiving.

Acts 20:35b NJB

Four Attitudes for Giving

1. Give _____willingly_____.

For if the willingness is there, the gift is acceptable according to what one has, not according to what he does not have.

2 Corinthians 8:12 NIV

Each man should give what he has decided in his heart to give, not reluctantly or under compulsion.

2 Corinthians 9:7 NIV

2. Give _____thankfully_____.

How can I repay the Lord for all his goodness to me?

Psalm 116:12 NIV

Everything comes from you, and we have given you only what comes from your hand.

1 Chronicles 29:14b NIV

3. Give _____joyfully_____.

God loves a cheerful giver.

2 Corinthians 9:7b NIV

4. Give _____expectantly_____.

Remember this: whoever sows sparingly will also reap sparingly, and whoever sows generously will also reap generously.

2 Corinthians 9:6 NIV

Just as you excel in everything—in faith, in speech, in knowledge, in complete earnestness and in your love for us—see that you also excel in this grace of giving.

2 Corinthians 8:7 NIV

DISCUSSION QUESTIONS

*1. Take a few minutes to share what your relationships in this group have meant to you.

2. What are some practical ways you can demonstrate your gratitude to God?

3. Jesus said it is better to give than receive. Share about a time you found this to be true in your own life. How did giving make you feel?

4. Why do you think generosity is so important to God?

Serve Together
10 minutes

*1. In this session we've talked about giving financially. But another way for us to give is through the use of our time. What can you do to continue serving your church together as a group?

2. One person in your group who has seen a need and seized the opportunity to meet it is your small group host. His or her leadership in your group has provided an example of using one's gifts to serve others. Take a few minutes to affirm your host. Focus on the character qualities, gifts, and talents he or she brings to your group. Thank your host for all of his or her hard work.

SHARE TOGETHER
10 minutes

*1. We want to encourage you to continue to develop the purpose of evangelism in your small group life. We pray your project will be the starting point of a lifestyle of service for your group and for you as an individual. Our hope is that you will look back after these forty days and not say, "Look what we did," but rather say, "Look what we started!" What can your group do to continue reaching out to your community with the love of Jesus Christ?

2. Pastor Rick would love to hear about your small group's ministry and outreach projects. Please email your stories to *stories@purposedrivenlife. com*. Thanks!

WORSHIP TOGETHER
15 minutes

*1. What has been the most important lesson you have learned through the *40 Days of Community* study? Have each member of the group share something that has been meaningful to him or her. Then offer prayers of thanks together for what God has done in your lives.

2. Close your time together by praying for each other's prayer requests. Recognize and celebrate any answered prayers from previous weeks. Record your prayer requests on the Small Group Prayer and Praise Report beginning on page 82 of this study guide.

Before You Leave

1. If you are planning to share your small group outreach story during your church's celebration service this coming weekend, take a few minutes to work out the details of your presentation.

2. We encourage you to have a party or picnic together—a time to focus on fellowship and celebrate what God has done throughout the last several weeks. This gathering is also a good opportunity to bring friends who might want to join your small group. It gives potential group members a non-threatening environment in which to get acquainted with the rest of you. Talk about this with your group: Set a date, time, and location, and decide what kind of food you will have.

3. If you haven't already done so, take some time now to talk about your future together as a small group. Where will you go from here? If you plan to continue meeting together, when and where will you meet? What will you study? Is there anything you want to do differently in your group life? We invite you to visit our website at *www.Saddleback-Resources.com* and check out our other video-based small group studies.

SMALL GROUP
RESOURCES

HELPS FOR HOSTS

TOP TEN IDEAS FOR HELPING YOUR GROUP SUCCEED

Congratulations! As the host of your small group, you have responded to the call to help shepherd Jesus' flock. Few other tasks in the family of God surpass the contribution you will be making.

On the DVD, you will find Helps for Hosts that offer insights and coaching for facilitating each week's session. Each Helps for Hosts feature is taught by Pastor Rick Warren and is three to five minutes long.

As you prepare to facilitate your group, whether it is one session or the entire series, here are a few additional thoughts to keep in mind. We encourage you to read and review these tips with each new discussion host before he or she leads.

1. **Remember you are not alone.** God knows everything about you, and he knew you would be asked to facilitate your group. Even though you may not feel ready, this is common for all good hosts. God promises, *"I will never leave you; I will never abandon you"* (Hebrews 13:5 TEV). Whether you are facilitating for one evening, several weeks, or a lifetime, you will be blessed as you serve.

2. **Don't try to do it alone.** Pray right now for God to help you build a healthy team. If you can enlist a cohost to help you shepherd the group, you will find your experience much richer. This is your chance to involve as many people as you can in building a healthy group. All you have to do is ask people to help. You'll be surprised at the response.

3. **Be friendly and be yourself.** God wants to use your unique gifts and temperament. Be sure to greet people at the door with a big smile ... this can set the mood for the whole gathering. Remember, they are taking as big a step as you are to show up at your house! Don't try to do things exactly like another host; do them in a way that fits you. Admit when you don't have an answer and apologize when you make a mistake. Your group will love you for it and you'll sleep better at night.

4. **Prepare for your meeting ahead of time.** Review the session and the video Helps for Hosts. Write down your responses to each question. Pay special attention to exercises that ask group members to do something other than engage in discussion. These exercises will help your group live what the Bible teaches, not just talk about it. If the exercise employs one of the items in the Small Group Resources section (such as the Group Guidelines), be sure to look over that item so you'll know how it works.

5. **Pray for your group members by name.** Before you begin your session, take a few moments and pray for each member by name. You may want to review the prayer list at least once a week. Ask God to use your time together to touch the heart of every person in your group. Expect God to lead you to whomever he wants you to encourage or challenge in a special way. If you listen, God will surely lead.

6. **When you ask a question, be patient.** Someone will eventually respond. Sometimes people need a moment or two of silence to think about the question. If silence doesn't bother you, it won't bother anyone else. After someone responds, affirm the response with a simple "thanks" or "great answer." Then ask, "How about somebody else?" or "Would someone who hasn't shared like to add anything?" Be sensitive to new people or reluctant members who aren't ready to say, pray, or do anything. If you give them a safe setting, they will blossom over time. If someone in your group is a wallflower who sits silently through every session, consider talking to them privately and encouraging them to participate. Let them know how important they are to you — that they are loved and appreciated, and that the group would value their input. Remember, still water often runs deep.

7. **Provide transitions between questions.** Ask if anyone would like to read the paragraph or Bible passage. Don't call on anyone, but ask for a volunteer, and then be patient until someone begins. Be sure to thank the person who reads aloud.

8. **Break into smaller groups occasionally.** The Grow Together and Worship Together sections provide good opportunities to break into smaller circles of three to five people. With a greater opportunity to talk in a small circle, people will connect more with the study, apply more quickly what they're learning, and ultimately get more out of their small group

experience. A small circle also encourages a quiet person to participate and tends to minimize the effects of a more vocal or dominant member.

Small circles are also helpful during prayer time. People who are unaccustomed to praying aloud will feel more comfortable trying it with just two or three others. Also, prayer requests won't take as much time, so circles will have more time to actually pray. When you gather back with the whole group, you can have one person from each circle briefly update everyone on the prayer requests from their subgroups. The other great aspect of subgrouping is that it fosters leadership development. As you ask people in the group to facilitate discussion or to lead a prayer circle, it gives them a small leadership step that can build their confidence.

9. **Rotate facilitators occasionally.** You may be perfectly capable of hosting each time, but you will help others grow in their faith and gifts if you give them opportunities to host the group.

10. **One final challenge** (for new or first-time hosts): Before your first opportunity to lead, read each of the six passages that follow as a devotional exercise to help prepare you with a shepherd's heart. Trust us on this one. If you do this, you will be more than ready for your first meeting.

    • **Matthew 9:36–38 (NIV)**
      When Jesus saw the crowds, he had compassion on them, because they were harassed and helpless, like sheep without a shepherd. Then he said to his disciples, "The harvest is plentiful but the workers are few. Ask the Lord of the harvest, therefore, to send out workers into his harvest field."

    • **John 10:14–15 (NIV)**
      "I am the good shepherd; I know my sheep and my sheep know me—just as the Father knows me and I know the Father—and I lay down my life for the sheep."

    • **1 Peter 5:2–4 (NIV)**
      Be shepherds of God's flock that is under your care, serving as overseers—not because you must, but because you are willing, as God wants you to be; not greedy for money, but eager to serve; not lording it over those entrusted to you, but being examples to the flock. And when the Chief Shepherd appears, you will receive the crown of glory that will never fade away.

- **Philippians 2:1–5 (NIV)**

  If you have any encouragement from being united with Christ, if any comfort from his love, if any fellowship with the Spirit, if any tenderness and compassion, then make my joy complete by being like-minded, having the same love, being one in spirit and purpose. Do nothing out of selfish ambition or vain conceit, but in humility consider others better than yourselves. Each of you should look not only to your own interests, but also to the interests of others. Your attitude should be the same as that of Jesus Christ.

- **Hebrews 10:23–25 (NIV)**

  Let us hold unswervingly to the hope we profess, for he who promised is faithful. And let us consider how we may spur one another on toward love and good deeds. Let us not give up meeting together, as some are in the habit of doing, but let us encourage one another—and all the more as you see the Day approaching.

- **1 Thessalonians 2:7, 8, 11–12 (NIV)**

  But we were gentle among you, like a mother caring for her little children. We loved you so much that we were delighted to share with you not only the gospel of God but our lives as well, because you had become so dear to us.... For you know that we dealt with each of you as a father deals with his own children, encouraging, comforting and urging you to live lives worthy of God, who calls you into his kingdom and glory.

Frequently Asked Questions

How long will this group meet?

Your *40 Days of Community* small group will meet for six weeks. We encourage your group to add a seventh session for a celebration. In your final session, each group member may decide if he or she desires to continue on for another study. At that time you may also want to do some informal evaluation, discuss your Group Guidelines, and decide which study you want to do next. We recommend you visit our Web site at *www.SaddlebackResources.com* for more video-based small group studies.

Who is the host?

The host is the person who coordinates and facilitates your group meetings. In addition to a host, we encourage you to select one or more group members to lead your group discussions. Several other responsibilities can be rotated, including refreshments, prayer requests, worship, or keeping up with those who miss a meeting. Shared ownership in the group helps everybody grow.

Where do we find new group members?

Recruiting new members can be a challenge for groups, especially new groups with just a few people, or existing groups that lose a few people along the way. We encourage you to use the Circles of Life diagram on page 81 of this study guide to brainstorm a list of people from your workplace, church, school, neighborhood, family, and so on. Then pray for the people on each member's list. Allow each member to invite several people from their list. Some groups fear that newcomers will interrupt the intimacy that members have built over time. However, groups that welcome newcomers generally gain strength with the infusion of new blood. Remember, the next person you add just might become a friend for eternity. Logistically, groups find different ways to add members. Some groups remain permanently open, while others choose to open periodically, such as at the beginning or end of a study. If your group becomes too large for easy, face-to-face conversations, you can subgroup, forming a second discussion group in another room.

How do we handle the child care needs in our group?

Child care needs must be handled very carefully. This is a sensitive issue. We suggest you seek creative solutions as a group. One common solution is to have the adults meet in the living room and share the cost of a babysitter (or two) who can be with the kids in another part of the house. Another popular option is to have one home for the kids and a second home (close by) for the adults. If desired, the adults could rotate the responsibility of providing a lesson for the kids. This last option is great with school-age kids and can be a huge blessing to families.

GROUP GUIDELINES

It's a good idea for every group to put words to their shared values, expectations, and commitments. Such guidelines will help you avoid unspoken agendas and unmet expectations. We recommend you discuss your guidelines during session one in order to lay the foundation for a healthy group experience. Feel free to modify anything that does not work for your group.

Clear Purpose   To grow healthy spiritual lives by building a healthy small group community

Group Attendance   Give priority to the group meeting (call if I am absent or late)

Safe Environment   To create a safe place where people can be heard and feel loved (no quick answers, snap judgments, or simple fixes)

Be Confidential   To keep anything that is shared strictly confidential and within the group

Conflict Resolution   To avoid gossip and to immediately resolve any concerns by following the principles of Matthew 18:15 – 17

Spiritual Health   To give group members permission to speak into my life and help me live a healthy, balanced spiritual life that is pleasing to God

Limit Our Freedom   To limit our freedom by not serving or consuming alcohol during small group meetings or events so as to avoid causing a weaker brother or sister to stumble (1 Corinthians 8:1 – 13; Romans 14:19 – 21)

Welcome Newcomers   To invite friends who might benefit from this study and warmly welcome newcomers

Building Relationships   To get to know the other members of the group and pray for them regularly

Other   _____

We have also discussed and agree on the following items:

- Child Care _____

- Starting Time _____

- Ending Time _____

If you haven't already done so, take a few minutes to fill out the Small Group Calendar on page 87.

CIRCLES OF LIFE

DISCOVER WHO YOU CAN CONNECT IN COMMUNITY

Use this chart to help carry out one of the values in the Group Guidelines, to "Welcome Newcomers."

"Follow me and I will make you fishers of men." (Matthew 4:19)

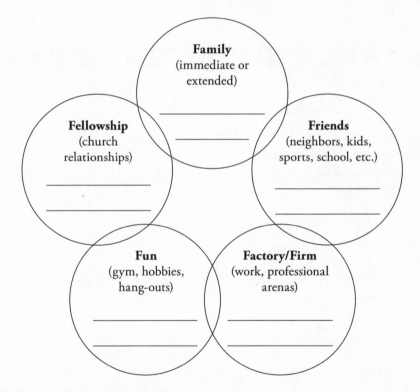

Follow this simple three-step process:

1. List one or two people in each circle.
2. Prayerfully select one person or couple from your list and tell your group about them.
3. Give them a call and invite them to your next meeting. Over 50 percent of those invited to a small group say, "Yes!"

SMALL GROUP PRAYER AND PRAISE REPORT

This is a place where you can write each other's requests for prayer. You can also make a note when God answers a prayer. Pray for each other's requests. If you're new to group prayer, it's okay to pray silently or to pray by using just one sentence: "God, please help _____ to _____."

Date	Person	Prayer Request	Praise Report

Date	Person	Prayer Request	Praise Report

Date	Person	Prayer Request	Praise Report

Date	Person	Prayer Request	Praise Report

Date	Person	Prayer Request	Praise Report

SMALL GROUP CALENDAR

Healthy groups share responsibilities and group ownership. It might take some time for this to develop. Shared ownership ensures that responsibility for the group doesn't fall to one person. Use the calendar to keep track of social events, mission projects, birthdays, or days off. Complete this calendar at your first or second meeting. Planning ahead will increase attendance and shared ownership.

Date	Lesson	Location	Facilitator	Snack or Meal
10/22	Session 2	Steve & Laura's	Bill Jones	John & Alice

Answer Key

Session One: What Matters Most

Nothing I <u>say</u> will matter.
Nothing I <u>know</u> will matter.
Nothing I <u>believe</u> will matter.
Nothing I <u>give</u> will matter.
Nothing I <u>accomplish</u> will matter.
Love is a <u>command</u>.
Love is a <u>choice</u>.
Love is a <u>conduct</u>.
Love is a <u>commitment</u>.

Session Two: Reaching Out Together

Recognize the <u>need</u>.
Take <u>inventory</u>.
Get <u>organized</u>.
Measure the <u>need</u>.
Prepare your <u>heart</u>.
Be <u>available</u>.

Session Three: Belonging Together

Love always <u>protects</u>.
Protects = <u>cover over with silence</u>
Love always <u>trusts</u>.
We believe <u>in</u> each other ... we believe <u>for</u> each other.
Love always <u>hopes</u>.
Be <u>enthusiastic</u> about other people's accomplishments.
Love always <u>perseveres</u>.

SESSION FOUR:
GROWING TOGETHER

Growing together requires <u>patience</u>.
Growing together requires <u>truthfulness</u>.
Check your <u>motives</u>.
Plan your <u>presentation</u>.
Plan <u>when</u> you'll say it.
Plan <u>what</u> you'll say.
Plan <u>how</u> you'll say it.
<u>Pray</u>.
Say it <u>tactfully</u>.
Say it <u>lovingly</u>.
Say it <u>gently</u>.
Growing together requires <u>forgiveness</u>.

SESSION FIVE:
SERVING TOGETHER

Make themselves <u>available</u> to serve.
Work as a <u>team</u>.
Think more about <u>others</u> than themselves.
Do every task with equal <u>dedication</u>.

SESSION SIX:
WORSHIPING TOGETHER

Giving makes me more like <u>God</u>.
Giving draws me <u>closer</u> to God.
Giving is the antidote to <u>materialism</u>.
Giving strengthens my <u>faith</u>.
Giving is an investment for <u>eternity</u>.
Giving blesses me in <u>return</u>.
Give <u>willingly</u>.
Give <u>thankfully</u>.
Give <u>joyfully</u>.
Give <u>expectantly</u>.

MY SMALL GROUP

ROSTER AND CONTACT
INFORMATION

	Name	Home Phone	Email
1.			
2.			
3.			
4.			
5.			
6.			
7.			
8.			
9.			
10.			
11.			
12.			
13.			
14.			

ADDITIONAL RESOURCES

The Purpose Driven Life
What on Earth Am I Here For?

You are not an accident. Even before the universe was created, God had you in mind, and he planned you for his purposes. These purposes extend far beyond the few years you will spend on earth. You were made to last forever!

This award-winning, internationally acclaimed book, read by more than 30 million people around the globe has changed the lives of countless people as they find a true relationship with their creator. By helping people discover that to find meaning and purpose, the only place to start is with God.

This book will help you understand why you are alive and God's amazing plan for you – both here and now, and for eternity. And knowing that purpose for your life will help reduce your stress, focus your energy, simplify your decisions, give meaning to your life, and, most importantly, prepare you for eternity.

This is a book of hope and challenge that you will read and re-read, offering more than 1,200 scriptural quotes and references, and inspiration to engage in God's plan for your life.

Available in hard and soft covers, audio CD, and leather-bound editions.

www.SaddlebackResources.com

The Purpose Driven Life
Six-session DVD-led Study

Throughout this six-session study, taught by Pastor Rick Warren, you will discover the answer to life's most fundamental questions, "What on Earth Am I Here For?"

This study, alongside the Purpose Driven Life book as part of the 40 Days of Purpose campaign, has been used by millions of people and thousands of churches worldwide since its release less than a decade ago. It will give you and your group the opportunity to discuss the implications and applications of living the life God created you to live.

Whether experiencing this spiritual adventure as a small group or on your own, this study will change your life and the way you view God's plan for it here on earth and afterwards.

40 Days of Love
Spiritual Growth Campaign

Uncover the core of Jesus' ministry in how we show love to the people God has placed in our lives. How can we communicate more like Jesus? How do we love our creator, our neighbors, and ourselves? Learn why love is patient, kind, forgiving, unselfish and always speaks the truth during this six-week journey into the heart of the matter.

The 40 Days of Love Campaign features:

+ Six studies by Pastor Rick Warren based on 1 Corinthians 13 (DVD video presentations and accompanying small group study guides).

+ *The Relationship Principles of Jesus*, the book by Pastor Tom Holladay, which addresses six relationship principles broken down into 40 daily readings.

+ Sermon transcripts, outlines and audio files for each of the six weeks of the campaign, plus promotional materials, and curriculum for Children and Youth.

> **"** Of all the commands in the Bible, two are the most important: Love God with all of your heart and love your neighbor as yourself. Above everything else we need to make love our number one priority, our primary objective, our life purpose. I can't tell you how excited I am about what will happen in your life, your family, and your friendships in this 40-day campaign. **"** *Rick*

Share Your Thoughts

With the Author: Your comments will be forwarded to the author when you send them to *zauthor@zondervan.com*.

With Zondervan: Submit your review of this book by writing to *zreview@zondervan.com*.

Free Online Resources at
www.zondervan.com

Zondervan AuthorTracker: Be notified whenever your favorite authors publish new books, go on tour, or post an update about what's happening in their lives at www.zondervan.com/authortracker.

Daily Bible Verses and Devotions: Enrich your life with daily Bible verses or devotions that help you start every morning focused on God. Visit www.zondervan.com/newsletters.

Free Email Publications: Sign up for newsletters on Christian living, academic resources, church ministry, fiction, children's resources, and more. Visit www.zondervan.com/newsletters.

Zondervan Bible Search: Find and compare Bible passages in a variety of translations at www.zondervanbiblesearch.com.

Other Benefits: Register to receive online benefits like coupons and special offers, or to participate in research.

ZONDERVAN.com/
AUTHORTRACKER
follow your favorite authors